LIKE MOST REVELATIONS

Other Books by Richard Howard

Poetry

Quantities   1962
The Damages   1967
Untitled Subjects   1969
Findings   1971
Two-Part Inventions   1974
Fellow Feelings   1976
Misgivings   1979
Lining Up   1983
No Traveller   1989

Criticism

Alone with America   1969
    (expanded edition 1980)
Preferences   1974

LIKE MOST REVELATIONS

New Poems by
Richard Howard

A Cornelia & Michael Bessie Book
Pantheon Books New York

All rights reserved under International and Pan-American Copyright Conventions.
Published in the United States by Pantheon Books, a division of Random House, Inc.,
New York.

The poems in this work were originally published as follows:

"Mademoiselle's Last Friday" in *Columbia College Today*, Fall 1991, Vol. 18, No. 3 ·
"After K452" in *The New Yorker*, July 1, 1991 · "Lives of the Painters—Artists' Antidotes" in *The New Yorker*, August 3, 1992 · "Undertakings" in *The New Yorker*, August
31, 1992 · "Homage" in *The New Theater Review* (Lincoln Center) #4 · "Like Most Revela-
tions" in *The Boston Phoenix Literary Section*, June 1991 · "To a Librettist at Liberty" in
Poetry, January 1992, Vol. CLIX, No. 4 · "A Lost Art" in *Poetry*, February 1993, Vol.
CLXI, No. 5 · "For James Boatwright, 1937–88" in *Western Humanities Review*, Winter
1988, Vol. XLII, No. 4 · "Centenary Peripateia . . ." in *Chelsea* 52 · "To the Tenth Muse:
A Recommendation" in *Southwest Review*, Autumn 1991, Vol. 76, No. 4 · "For David
Kalstone, 1932–86" in *Raritan Review*, Spring 1991, Vol. X, No. 4 · ". . . Et Dona Fe-
rentes" in *Raritan Review*, Spring 1989, Vol. 8, No. 4 · "Man Who Beat Up Homosexuals
Reported to Have AIDS Virus" in *Salmagundi*, Winter 1992, No. 93 · "Writing Off" in
Partisan Review, Fall 1991, Vol. LVIII, No. 4 · "Poem Beginning with a Line by Isadora
Duncan" in *Partisan Review*, Summer 1989, Vol. LV, No. 3 · "What Word Did the
Greeks Have for It?" in *The Threepenny Review*, Fall 1990, No. 43 · "And Tell Sad Stories"
in *The Yale Review*, Vol. 79, No. 4 · "Culture and Its Misapprehensions III" in *The Yale
Review*, July 1992, Vol. 80, No. 3 · "For Matthew Ward, 1951–90" in *The Kenyon Review*,
New Series, Spring 1991, Vol. XIII, No. 2 · "Theory of Flight: 1908" in *The Kenyon Re-
view*, New Series, Winter 1990, Vol. XII, No. 1 · "Occupations" in *The Kenyon Review*,
New Series, Fall 1992 · "A Beatification" in *Grand Street*, Winter 1990, Vol. 9, No. 2 ·
"The Victor Vanquished" in *Antaeus*, Spring/Autumn 1990, Vol. 64/65 · "Visitations"
in *Michigan Quarterly Review*, Fall 1993, Vol. 32, No. 4 · "For Robert Phelps, Dead at 66"
in *The New Republic*, November 6, 1989.

Library of Congress Cataloging-in-Publication Data

Howard, Richard, 1929–
Like most revelations : new poems / by Richard Howard.
    p.   cm.
"A Cornelia & Michael Bessie book."
ISBN 0-679-43163-2
I. Title.
PS3558.08826L49   1994
811'.54—dc20   93-34157   CIP

Book Design by M. Kristen Bearse

Manufactured in the United States of America

First Edition

9 8 7 6 5 4 3 2 1

Cum tacent, clamant

—Cicero

Contents

LIKE MOST REVELATIONS

Like Most Revelations

after Morris Louis

It is the movement that incites the form,
discovered as a downward rapture—yes,
it is the movement that delights the form,
sustained by its own velocity. And yet

it is the movement that delays the form
while darkness slows and encumbers; in fact
it is the movement that betrays the form,
baffled in such toils of ease, until

it is the movement that deceives the form,
beguiling our attention—we supposed
it is the movement that achieves the form.
Were we mistaken? What does it matter if

it is the movement that negates the form?
Even though we give (give up) ourselves
to this mortal process of continuing,
it is the movement that creates the form.

Occupations

for David Alexander

Of course we're still using the old stationery—who can find paper these days?—but as you see, the lettering outside has already been changed, and to all intents and purposes this is now the Galerie Millon (I was Mathilde Millon before the late M. Bernheim married me). And I believe the Reichsmarschall will find that nothing shown him is on the list of Proscribed Artists. May I call your attention to these—no, not the very recent things: anything begun since 1942 I find a bit too stiff (no doubt the rigidity of an intimated end), but a choice among the later canvases, my dear Reichsmarschall . . . After all, the man is well into his seventies, and we may call anything done in the last decade a late work, wouldn't you say? Though the gallery has represented Bonnard since . . . oh goodness, since before my marriage, these paintings have just reached us. The old fellow keeps them ever so long in his studio, down there at Le Cannet, endlessly reworking what I feel to be the lessons he has learned—you see, here? and over here, particularly—from his friend Matisse.

8 January
42. Le Cannet.

Dear Matisse, I have sad news:
Marthe has died—of what she called
her "immortal disease." . . . First the lungs
were attacked, then the digestive tract,
yet she managed to survive each new onset

for all the pain she must have been suffering,
   until at last, just six days ago,
    the heart gave out. We laid her to rest
      in the graveyard I can see
      from upstairs at Le Bosquet:
        a comfort to me,
        knowing she is there . . .
           I think you recall
           the strange delusion:
    unclean! Marthe unclean!—which kept
    her so many hours immersed
   in the bath. We had made it a joke
  between us—very nearly a joke,
enough of one for me to paint her there,
how many times? A modern Naiad, or as
  Monet would have said, a nenuphar!
  Our little ceremony for Marthe
      brought back the time, can it be
      twenty years? when Vuillard and I
        and old Clemenceau
        laid Monet to rest . . .
           So much of life is
           buried already!

Just consider this delightful view of a mimosa tree from the studio window, for example: it was begun in 1939, along with other momentous enterprises, if I may say so, and not finished (though what works by this painter can ever be called finished?)—not released, then, until only a few weeks ago, when the old fellow himself had the canvas sent to me directly. We may sell it along with these others—thank goodness he is exempt from the Doctrinal Tests, though like Matisse and Dufy not considered "meritorious." . . .

All the same I still believe
in reality, the way
Cézanne believed in it—I believe
in repetition, that is, and I am
at work on some new views of the Bay. . . . They must
be new, because every day I see different
things, or I see things differently:
the sky, the fields, the water beyond,
    it all keeps changing, you could
    drown in the differences.
        Yet that is just what
        keeps us alive, no?
            Despite our bad skies,
            how the spring responds!
    Daily on my walks, some new
    species of flower appears—
as if each one were having its turn!
this morning the first almond blossoms,
like proclamations attached to the bare trees
(a kind of bravery, I can't help thinking)
and soon the mimosas will begin
to set yellow pennants in the woods,
    as if it was a signal!
    Of course everything begins
        on the ground and moves
        up, but I see things
            best against the light. . . .

*I can let you have such work in lots, at a most attractive rate for the whole
group here in the gallery. . . . Amusing, by the way, that barely perceptible
woman's face down there on the left, yes, at the very bottom, almost
drowned out by the light. She is looking up the stairs toward the painter,
not out the window at all, where the mimosa suffuses the whole picture*

*with gold, filling the window so that it has something of the appearance of
stained glass. . . .*

                  the horizon lies
        much lower in my landscapes
        than it ever did before. . . .
You know, at our age, we tend—except
for P, of course, who is hardly one of us—
to be more interested in objects than in
        the construction of the universe.
These encroachments, these occupations—
        by disease, by sorrow, by
        the Germans—come in great waves,
            you know what I mean:
            that thing old Rodin
                always used to say,
                about how it takes
        an exceptional array
        of circumstances to grant
    a man seventy years of life and
    the luck to keep doing what he loves.
Oh, the waves come, they keep coming over us,
and though we may be nearly drowned, they leave us
        just where we were, and we know that if
    they are strong, we are even stronger,
        for they pass, and we remain . . .
        "Old Rodin": what insolence,
            my calling him that!
        we're both much older
                than he lived to be,
                pontificating
    in front of the Gates of Hell
        —remember those afternoons

in the rue de Varennes, lecturing
overdressed women in his garden. . . .
Did you ever believe we would be that old?

*Such a pleasure, my dear Reichsmarschall, indeed a privilege, to be able to
offer these canvases for actual purchase. Only last May, you know—we
were obliged to destroy—in the courtyard of the Louvre!—some five hundred pictures by Masson, Léger, poor old Kisling, even Picasso, really horrors—all canvases entirely unfit for sale. The fire went on all day, and
the smoke covered the sky, even the next morning . . .*

27 February.
Dear Matisse,

It is not easy, keeping abreast
of events, nor have I any great
            longing to know what may be
happening in the world, I
            almost said the real
            world. Don't believe that.
                  A few days ago
                  I learned about Joss—
not how he died, just his death.
All that *l'Eclaireur de Nice*
reports is that he had been "ailing." . . .
Over forty years since Bernheim-Jeune
took me on, you must have come to the gallery
soon after—about nineteen hundred and nine?
What a long time Joss did the one thing!
Most people are not conscious enough
            to exult in monotony,
            but perhaps God is—perhaps

God says each morning
to the moon: "Encore!"
I know that is what
Joss would say to me
whenever a show came down.
And today, inside black borders,
Mathilde Bernheim writes to say she is
asking "his" painters to testify—
you must have had the same letter—to what Joss
has accomplished for "Independent French Art."
She thinks this will save her family
from the persecutions. . . . I was glad
to write, as you must have been,
and Dufy, Rouault, Derain. . . .
But to tell the truth
none of this will do
the least bit of good.

*I am so happy to know that this lot is passing to such appreciative hands,
and eyes, of course. Is it not charming, the woman at her toilette, seen as if
by accident through the doorway? Wonderful, that in these dark times
the painter could find so much light to celebrate, such depths to plumb so
brilliantly!*

Dear Matisse, you know
as well as I: the Germans
acknowledge a single name
among "French" painters. Our conquerors
recognize only our conqueror,
if I may put it that way—perhaps you see
Monsieur Picasso as no such thing, Matisse,
but I have textual evidence
as to how that Spaniard has seen me.
"I like him best, your Bonnard,"

he once wrote Joss (who of course
passed on this good news)
"when he is not thinking
of being a painter,
when his canvases
are full of literature"
—this is really what he said—
"rotten with anecdotes." Did that suffice?
Not for our Pablo. Kahnweiler was
kind enough to send the latest bulletin,
and I am compelled to copy it out here
for your edification—one way
to exorcise the curse of the thing,
or so I hope: "What he does
is not painting—he never
goes beyond his own
sensibility.
He doesn't know how
to choose. Take his sky—
first he paints blue, more or less
the way it looks. Then he looks
a while longer and sees mauve in it,
so he adds a touch or two of mauve,
just to be sure. Then he assumes there may be
a little pink there too—why not add some pink?
If he looks long enough he'll wind up
adding a little yellow, instead
of deciding what color
the sky really ought to be.
Is that painting? No,
that's taking advice
from Nature, asking
her to supply you

with information: Bonnard
obeys Nature! another
decadent, the end of an old idea. . . ."

There you have the words, my dear Matisse,
of a fellow artist, a practitioner
of the *métier* we have shared, all of us
    for how many years? Is this the man
    I can ask to speak to Herr Abetz
        on behalf of Joss Bernheim—
        and of Mathilde Bernheim?
            If you can do it,
            I leave it to you.

Very well, we shall send the entire shipment to your private car at the gare de l'Est. Two cars? All the better! And the bill to the Einsatzstab Rosenberg. No, no, all these have come to us from the artist himself—not one from other dealers. Graf Metternich was at some pains to stipulate: the stock of Seligmann, Wildenstein, Loeb, e tutti quanti *must be transferred to the Embassy as a security for eventual peace negotiations. I understand perfectly.*

                    . . . After yesterday
                    I belong, once more,
            to the human race—a trial
            member, but a member still,
        all because they have decided to
        operate: the surgeon has bestowed
civil status, even a country, on me:
my country is The Hospital, and I am
        Dr A's patient in Room 14,
        on whom Dr B will operate.
            The corridor where I walk
            and wait and write this to you
                is my realm; no one

dreams of disputing
the territory.
I see other men,
and women too, who have been
operated on, brought back
on their gurneys, the surgeons, interns
and nurses clustering around them
like white flies. Through their doors I can hear the groans
these patients make, even in their sleep, the same
groans I shall make, when it is my turn.
The nurses know me, and I know them:
one comes for "temperature,"
one for "blood," and another
with "pills." The pill nurse
is pretty, the rest
are young. When I walk
past their glassed-in booth
I always hear them talking
about us, their patients. Theirs.
And for the first time in a long while
I find humanity better than
I had supposed. Now I can more easily
regard my own death, which no longer divides
me from the world. It is possible,
nothing more. It becomes a simple
statistic. In rooms off this
corridor, a percentage
of patients must die,
and this percentage
is what they attempt
to reduce. Each nurse
in this wing will regard my
death as her failure—the one
who looks like Danielle Darrieux's

daughter says that after each "deceased"
she won't sleep for a week. My death no longer
exposes me to the living. That is why
    I have made my will so easily
    and told my notary where to find
        the pictures I had hidden
        so long. I have forgotten
            nothing, for it seems
            only fair to meet
                with an attentive
                precision the same
        precision they devote to
        my file, from which no X-ray,
blood-analysis, or fever-chart
is missing. I too want to present
the anesthesiologist with a man
according to the rules. But once you obey
    the rules, there is nothing left to do
    but wait. I wait. And I look for what
        it could mean, this death of mine
        that seems so near. I admit
        I will be nothing
        (otherwise death is
            not death, and even
            one's thoughts about it
        are just playing with words). And
        without my body, what is
    left of me? No reading the paper,
    no talk with the doctor making rounds.
No action of any kind. But do I make
these actions I assume I am making now?
    It is my newspaper, printed in
    an edition of thousands, that puts
        pressure on me to read it;

the doctor comes when he feels
like coming, evades
my questions, departs:
there is my freedom.
Which is nothing but
my uncertainty about
what is going to happen
next. Of course, that is my freedom, but
having been introduced into this
vast machinery, I am not even sure
such uncertainty as to my fate is part
and parcel of my life—my death is
not enough to dispel it. No doubt
I am the total of my
memories and nothing else,
that huge collection
gathered by my life
and dispersed by my
death. But so many
of these memories—I see
now they don't belong to me . . .
What did I do that was mine? I went
to the parish school, served out my term
in the infantry—and I was not alone.
In each photograph I belong to a group,
and someone must draw a little cross
over my head if I am to be
identified. Dear Matisse,
nothing is there. What remains
is the almond tree
I was working on
the morning I came
to the hospital.

Pray God it will be there still
if I am allowed to go home. . . .

Of course we have carefully weeded out all the identifiable portraits: in the Bonnard lot there were a number of studies of my late husband and his family, his friends. They were obliged to join the others in three requisitioned rooms in the Louvre, where as you know they were slashed to ribbons by members of the Einsatzstab themselves—a regrettable procedure, but apparently a necessary one. You know, my dear Reichsmarschall, we French have an old poem which I always like to recite in times like these:

I claim the right to act as if
the War were an old dog sitting
at the lovely feet of our France. . . .

Poem Beginning with a Line by Isadora Duncan

The third time I resisted D'Annunzio
was years after the War,
and to dilapidations in My Life
    every limb testifies
since the escapes (elementary enough)
    of those Houdini days!
I find it pitiful to contemplate
    our mutual conceit
on those absurd occasions, now we know
    all that has intervened.
Yet what *do* we know, really? I say "all"
    as if I had been schooled
in catastrophe, when Triumph was my mode.
    His too, apparently . . .

Raising his eyelids as though he were
    removing his trousers,
the poet stood in my Paris *loge d'artiste,*
    towering under me,
the *chaise-longue* crammed with his chrysanthemums
    —"lion blooms," he called them,
"Ecco i leoni"—and licked his lips as if
    they were someone else's.
That was my first evasion: "They smell—" I said,
    "they smell like drowned sailors."
Whereupon virtue was intact: Italians are

grimly conventional—
so much easier to shock than to persuade.
    The next time, my escape

was dicier, for in his own domain . . .
    I was dancing in Rome,
and what occurred, or failed to, at the hotel
    was not, as I recall,
the outcome of odious comparisons merely,
    but of actions: the sheets
were thrown back, and Gabriele showed
    a sincere if brackish
enthusiasm for my thighs—"columns more
    melodious by night
than Memnon's temple at dawn"—and just then
    Deucie, my Doberman,

leaped on the bed, wild in my defence
    or was it my defeat?—
another jealous bitch like the Marchesa Casati!
    But could a dog deter
that lover at that point? It was my own
    screams of "Deucie, down!"
which shrivelled my assailant to his doom
    as only memory can:
Deucie—Duse: mine as much as his
    the disgrace awakened,
in a sacred name consigned to comedy,
    the fiasco of farce—
laughter has no erectile tendencies:
    Deucie and I were saved. . . .

In Nice, too, that *third* time (counting was
    a crucial part of it)

even desire, for him, was out of the question
      without the distractions
of vanity. And love impossible. He would be
      entitled only to
lies and funny business, and so I fell
      or would have fallen yet
again, if it had not been for the odd crystals,
      powders, grains, the uncut
gems and a thousand gorgeous trifles poured
      for the sake of "aura,"
some burnt, some merely glowing like embers
      around us where we lounged

in that silly mummy-case of an apartment—
      another hour there and I
should have died in the odor of Orient
      as some are said to die
in the odor of sanctity. Did *I* say as much?
      I must have—the remark
made his eyebrows play like summer lightning
      up around his hairline
(bald as an egg, but he has a hairline still).
      Checkmate! I've learned it means
Shah mat: the king is dead. Such artifice
      was bound to spring a leak.
Out cold, bequeathing me a carcass quite
      uninhabitable . . .

My resistances, as I have called them, were
      no more than submissions
to Animal, Vegetable, Mineral Realms—
      flower, dog, druggery.
I wonder how to escape, were he to press
      new designs that must be

obscene to be believed? Trust inertia
    over the intellect
I cannot muster . . . At least it makes a tale,
    a sort of haphazard
Scheherazade. And if we were never amazed,
    there would be no stories
to tell about us. Believe in the mystery
    of Woman: it gives her one.

Centenary Peripeteia and Anagnoresis
Beginning with a Line by Henry James

"The accent of Massachusetts rings up and down the Grand
Canal, and the bark of Chicago disturbs the siesta." This final
phrase could almost be the opening verse of a poem. I com-
mend it to the insomniac among you as an exercise for the small
hours, to complete this haunting refrain.

—A. N. Wilson

The bark of Chicago disturbs the siesta,
Oporto resounds to an Omaha twang;
Manhattan has taken Menton for its oyster,

the Via Condotti is clogged with a throng
of midwestern couples (in matching Bermudas)
whose vowels are strident, whose consonants sting.

Possessed of the touch—and the temper!—of Midas,
our tourists have tended, these last hundred years,
to make the Hesperides something like Hades:

also sprach Henry James. Now behold the reverse
situation abroad in our land: Arab glottals
astonish the ears of Fort Worth, and the ores

of Missoula as well as the firs of Seattle
are raucously bid for by Japanese throats;
commercial Miami is known as a "Little

Caracas," where Spanish is queen of the streets;
from seedy Las Vegas to Saudi La Costa,
our enterprise echoes to "Frogs, Wogs and Brits,"

according to Lyndon LaRouche, a disaster
to some and to such, yet a wiser man learns
to lend a deaf ear to this chauvinist bluster:

in history's prospect the Screw always Turns
now this way now that, in the words of the Master;
and he who exults must become he who mourns.

For Matthew Ward, 1951–90

*who stipulated that I speak, at
a memorial service, of his
"professional development,"
halted by AIDS*

Out of the doorway, on a Soho street
where I had no reason for being (so I thought),
you stepped and stopped me, murmuring my name,
then yours, as if to rhyme—as if a tryst
had long since been agreed upon and drawn
                    us both together
on an autumn evening, eleven years ago.
Together? I wonder. The lure was not to be
my Going Inclination of those years,
nor you the boy I greedily took you for—
as if the eagle had regained Olympus with
                    the wrong Ganymede!
True, I would find you finicky to a fault—
you had been expertly tutored to serve Mass,
not empty ashtrays. Denver, Dublin, nuns
had worked their will, and by the time we met
your mind was a kind of sieve—the finer the mesh,
                    the more it rejects!
Language, not love, was our only covenant;
no way to go unless it was This Way Out.
So together (at last!) we undertook a search
for the Just Word—translating, in your case,

being one more escape (that's what the verb
means—*getting across*)
out of the frying pan into . . . an empty grate.
Eagerly, though, you began with Roland Barthes
whose *Fashion System* certified you had
a certain sour felicity of phrase,
and as far as I could tell—the interval
was evanescent—
you had invented your living, if not your life . . .
Of course there were aggravations—perhaps the one
comfort I could give was this advice:
when Frenchmen talk, don't lift the needle off
the record, it will only go back by itself
to the beginning.
And there *were* fulfillments. If you loved
the toils of such an enterprise
more than others love its low rewards,
you would be blessed by the paradox of form:
insides are always larger than outsides. Meursault
in *your* voice sounded
much too good to be a good translation—
not the absence of thinking but its end;
in the scruple of *your* lexicon Colette
showed less anxiety about civilized things
than optimism about the savage ones:
this you did not share,
yet showed it to be hers. You were, after all,
a friend to women and a lover of men.
Whereby came the horror, and a call
at midnight to announce, in tears, your doom.
Diagnosis loomed as the commonest disease,
and you decided
to learn for yourself. You would make your life
your argument, decamping at thirty-nine

like Schweitzer for the darkest continent
and a hospital. You argued against your friends,
for sickness tries to shrink the world to itself,
               and we were what world
you had. No need, you told us from the first,
to be afraid of death—*you* wouldn't be there
when that occurred. The twenty friends who were,
watching you disappear before you died—
loss by daily loss—were quite afraid,
               and with good reason:
how could you forgive such presences
when you would soon be gone? Jesus said
Forgive our enemies—nothing about our friends . . .
Matthew, I speak unforgiven, having no wish
to commemorate you in your accomplishments,
               though forced to do so
by your dying writ. Our gifts belong to the world,
whether avowed or privately bestowed;
but our failings—all that we cannot give away—
belong to those who love us, those we love.
And though I come to praise your enterprise
               (which is mine as well),
I offer in parting no praise for your success,
nor pride in the promise of your career. I claim
no more than what, if you loved me, is my share
of your folly, your madness, your sickness and your death.
That is all I have of you and all
               a lover deserves.

Mademoiselle's Last Friday

In Memoriam H.N.

. . . Nothing irregular about it.
The many years I have been in his employ,
  he repeatedly gave evidence of
entire and indeed eager satisfaction,

  once even assured me I was his
"irreplaceable" means of self-expression.
  Madame, you see, was never on hand—
she gardens in all weathers. When a woman

  goes out in the pouring rain to brush
caterpillars off rose trees, one may conceive
  as a general rule that life indoors
leaves something to be desired, for all parties.

  To me he dictated his works, walking
not back and forth, nor up and down, but in
  and out of his particular rhythm
—the body has a mind of its own, he once

  asserted when I could scarcely hear
pronouncements uttered from what might be called
  the apogee of his orbit. Soon
I learned to make out his sentences *en route,*

letting the preened compositions . . . come,
my part in them a matter of pride to me,
    and mere practicality to him.
This was our program for nearly two decades

    during which "we," if I may say so,
were accorded the Prix Goncourt and crowned
    (the term is purely figurative)
by the Académie-Française more than once.

    Lately our procedure had altered:
for a few hours each day I would read to him,
    —he lay on a couch with his eyes closed—
from his own writings. This was his great passion:

    to hear himself *pronounced* by someone
else. He would listen, apparently entranced,
    sometimes nodding, sometimes grimacing,
and occasionally murmur a few words

    (I always took it down). Once he said:
"We are not descended from the ape, but are
    returning to him in great haste," and
during another of these somnolences:

    "So splendid were the castles I built
myself in Spain that even their ruins suffice."
    More and more frequently he would fall
into a torpor, no longer listening

    even to devices of his own
so highly prized, though I went on reading
    as he had asked me to, words falling
out of one solitude into another,

but I never left him till I had
waited the silence out, wanting to be sure
    there was nothing further to record.
It was not difficult to fix the moment

    when neither of us needed to speak
anymore. And it is absurd to require
    your presence merely to ascertain
there was nothing irregular, as you call it,

    about his death—he just slid away
from himself. Madame is wrong to reproach me
    —me, of all people!—with negligence,
I was quite attentive all the while he died

    —after all, he was dying every day
as well as just now: where was she then?
    I have typed up what I could decipher
of our last few sessions' phrases, but in fact

    all he wanted today was to hear
himself out. I met that requirement as well,
    and I trust, Inspector, that I am
free to go now? Thank you. Yes, I know my way.

A Lost Art

Vienna, 1805

There is no ceremony to stand on,
just walk in! No call to be dismayed:
it is not chaos you see in my shop,
but the leavings of creation; nothing
can do you any harm, and nothing is
so far along that you'll do harm to *it* . . .

Suppose you sit—just put that on the floor—
over here . . . Never mind, I can fix it:
legs are the least of my difficulties,
there! Welcome to the land of the missing,
where little is past recall. Or repair.
This? Oh, this is my *first* capybara,

I persuaded a chamberlain I know
at the Palace—whom you may know as well,
he's been up there for years, for *dynasties:*
Herr Pufendorf?—to let me have it back,
once I had pledged myself to substitute
a more convincing representative.

No, no, the eyes are set too high, and *green*!
a libel on the living article . . .
I keep it here, fallacious as it is,
to remind me, in a cautionary way,

that I can do (and have done) better work.
I have long since eclipsed such things, rising

from capybara to *homo capax:*
honest progress. A pity you cannot
confirm my boast; a word to Pufendorf,
not so long since, would have afforded you
the sight of my *magnum opus,* displayed
in the Imperial Museum—kept out

for years, just standing there in . . . state,
I have been told, in spite of protests from
the poor man's family. Not Pufendorf—
he has no family, to my knowledge!
"Poor man" refers to our black Angelo
Solyman, who was to be seen entire,

naked from head to heels, and all between,
the upshot of my labor and my skill . . .
It would have been no trick at all to do
a costumed figure, just the face and hands
set off by the white court dress, the gold braid,
the medals he wore invariably wore;

quite another matter to show the man's . . .
manhood, as my commission specified;
why, just to gain possession of the corpse
was a crime! Or would have been, if I'd
been caught: stolen at birth, stolen at death—
a slave's fate, for all the honors bestowed.

Then came the wife's compunction—she had been
widowed by a Flemish general and
married to Solyman in secret rite,

though in St. Stephen's Cathedral. Yet
not even the Cardinal-Archbishop
could baffle the Emperor's plan. And I?

I did as I was ordered, did my best:
I allude to the *new* Emperor, of course,
not our late Joseph, who abhorred the sight
of stuffed animals of any species
(the entire Imperial family
suffered from this . . . susceptibility,

until Francis—in so many respects
the converse of his uncle). Now Francis,
Solyman safely dead, commanded me
to prepare, preserve, and present him
as a perfect specimen *in all respects.*
He meant, of course, *in one:* I was to find

a way of representing what is held
to be the special virtue of black men,
although, however . . . outstanding in life,
our man's endowments were, most likely, dimmed
by being dead, revived in part, and stuffed!
Moreover he had died quite civilly—

no evidence from the gibbet would grant
a hint of eventual scope to my art
nor any sculptor's manual of scale
suggest a means of reckoning how much
I might have to contend with. And I could
hardly ask the wronged widow for details!

An old cookery book delivered me:
by gently passing oil of cloves, it said,

over the affected body parts . . . Well,
even in the coldest larder, it seems,
an ox's member could be coaxed to life
or at least to life's dimensions, for a while.

And so it came about that Solyman—
born a prince in Pangusitlong, raised
a slave by robbers in Messina, sold
to one General Lobkowitz, by whom
he was bequeathed to Prince von Liechtenstein
who freed and later pensioned him for life—

a Mason, moreover, in Mozart's Lodge
(where both attended assiduously!)
who spoke German, Italian, English, French,
an excellent player of faro and chess,
observed in Frankfurt by the adolescent
Goethe at the Emperor's election—

this very Solyman you might have seen
for yourself in all his mortifying
splendor in the Museum, though of course
what I had studied to produce was more
of a demonstration piece—much visited
by our ladies, and some gentlemen too!—

than any emblem of human headway
in what civilization we may have—
something by way of a memorandum,
actually. No, I never visited:
I did the work, it is gone. Why torment
myself further? I know what I achieved.

I am told that after the bombardment
(though before Bonaparte entered the town)
the thing—my masterpiece!—was stolen
from its case by old Countess Zacharoff
and later vanished in the deplorable
looting of the Zacharoff residence . . .

And Tell Sad Stories

Many of us, inexorably
subservient to your cool evasions,
    found them more flattering than candor
could ever be: you made it seem naive
    to inquire further. I wonder still
whether anything so crude as a question
    —"Donald, can we talk about ourselves?"—
might have cleared the reef on which intimacy
    founders. Nor in all your inventions

    (I have read them all) is the secret
ever betrayed: how you managed to compel
    Caliban appetites—which despise
sex and live for it (a form of suicide)—
    to serve an Ariel art. By the book,
delight seemed to be your exclusive *métier*,
    underpinning all experience:
an elation in the self *no matter what*.
    Oh, we guessed there must be something more,

    or something other—catacomb words
which remain alien to the text, unsaid.
    But all that unknown territory
is sealed off now, dark there. Even dark, we could
    detect the coercion of cadence;

"Some falls are anything but free," was my first
   thought upon finding you gaunt, sober,
smokeless, angry that life, if it was to be
   life at all, forced such relinquishings.

   "Choked, chastened—changed!" I marveled, hoping
I too had changed, else how could friendship survive?
   It would be Freud's old joke once again,
which so grimly cajoles our will: two Jews meet
   in the street. "Cohen, good to see you,
but how you've changed! You used to be a tall man,
   now look at you . . . You weren't bald before,
what happened to your hair? . . ." "But my name isn't Cohen . . ."
   "So, you've changed your name too!" We succumb

   to recognition, its sealing powers.
Must real life be the life one does not lead?
   Proof there is no sterner moralist
than pleasure, you were exiled from Paradise
   to the one country—your own—where you
were not a prophet. In that partial *patrie*
   —you were my friend, I was never yours—
the text impersonates the author. Your absence
   remains a mode of creating life.

Writing Off

All participation in art is based on the existence of others.

—Hebbel

"In a field I am," our latest laureate
        divulges, "the absence of field,"
content, if not resolved, to be missing
        in action, missing in passion—
forsaking as a form of *being there*!

To live on nothing is one theorem
        which Thoreau would have understood;
and not only to live on it, to let
        Nothing do our living for us . . .
It is the converse claim I wish to lodge,

a premise that we are because we make
        some sign of presence, all
that is signified by the marvellous
        post-juridical compound
self-evident. The claim is likely

to be clamorous, uncivil, often
        sacrilegious in its effects
(hence the tendency to label it
        at minimum a misdemeanor,
more likely a mania). I refer

to the patently incorrigible
        yen to inscribe our handiwork,
or rather the play of our hands, upon
        whatever amplitude is bare
enough to enable our disclosure.

As a rule the billboards are not put up
        to put up with our marauding,
and it is a tribute to the discretion
        of our poet's heretical
heroism that he scores identity

by absconding the evidence of it,
        withdrawing himself from the scene.
Most of us are not like that. We require
        a signature; KILROY WAS HERE
we scratch on the fresh paint, and sigh

with authorial satisfaction. Now
        behold the field from which Mark Strand
proclaims himself absent: here is a wall
        and at its base a ruined car
filled with spray-cans that strew the ground as well,

and every inch of wall and car and ground
        is covered, cancelled, *encrusted*
with the spirit-writing known as graffito,
        cursive abuse, cacography
which by its very glut becomes glamor,

a collaborative chaos of uncials,
        illegible and thus elect.

According to Erdmann (*Arabische Schriftkunst
            als Ornamente,* Bonn, 1910)
"Writing is one form of art in general

  whose aesthetic aspect is often so
            hypertrophied as to neglect
its chief purpose as communication . . .
            Horror vacui is of great
influence in the arrangement of signs."

Erdmann is right. The walls cannot be read
            as anything but palimpsest,
elemental commands made vacuous
            by the subsequent autograph
of those who obeyed them. Writing alone

appears to count, a thousand words worth no
            picture, "graphic," as we observe:
the quenched car is so tangled in a scurf
            of scribbles (the moving finger
having writ) that waves seem to have broken

over the ravaged and obviously tireless
            machine in opalescent foam,
a sea of troubles unopposed, unended . . .
            Bonnard, who could never leave off
retouching his canvases, would envy

these scaling laminations, pellicles
            of self-assertion which has turned
anonymous by superfetation. Here
            perhaps our laureate is met,
for these scriveners have made something

occasioned only when no one member
        conspicuously functions
in the field—repressed *and* represented
        by unspecifiable rinds
and flakes. (How many times we must peruse

these depths before the deepest impulse floats
        to the surface and is legible:
the inenarrable FUCK which appears
        only after the eye has long
frequented more decorous instances!)

Theirs is a polypoid scheme—a structure
        of self-immolating moilers
(like the pyramids and the cathedrals)
        wreaked upon the carapace of
what pyramids and cathedrals we have . . .

But for all the luscious integument,
        a variorum of texture
any post-impressionist might covet,
        is it meant to be seen? The wall,
the filthy field, the gutted car engorged

with the spray-cans which have given their all
        are unknown to view, closeted
from the eagerest archeologist
        of our cities' decline and fall.
Only a fluke snapshot insists: *this was,*

and my words, irresolute witness to
        such performance. I used to think
graffiti meant nothing but insolence,
        the mean and meager vandalism
which was all *ressentiment* could muster,

yet the wasted splendor of an empty
        lot in East Los Angeles
redefines the state of the art: how much
        of the world's making was never
intended for human eyes! Luxor, Lascaux,

sacred places where we learn we can change
        our faith without changing gods (and
vice versa) . . . To which I add the image
        of an unvisitable shrine
where obscure artisans have succeeded

in transcending the five destinies
        by which we claim to be guided:
mind body nation language home. This is
        how we learn, by just such unseen
art, to approach the divine. Next slide please.

For Robert Phelps, Dead at 66

The Times reports six years in Elyria,
    browbeaten suburb of your childhood
before my own had begun in Shaker Heights,
    the brighter side of Cleveland's tracks . . .

years I never took into account, nonplussed
    by your habit of addressing me
—or any other man you regarded as
    worthy of the gaudy attention

to bookish leanings and upstanding looks
    you were gaily ready to bestow—
as "my dear boy," "my son," and "my child," although
    you were clearly the one to be raised

—or lowered—to the permanently askew
    level of our promiscuities;
it became entertainment, "telling Robert"
    last night's scurrilous episode

and watching your vicarious blush appear,
    followed by the squeal of gratified
incredulity which greeted each disgrace . . .
    Oneself is always an abstraction—

le concret, ce sont les autres. To which end
   you listened more intently, waiting
like some credulous minotaur in his cave
   for Theseus to arrive, whereupon

you became Ariadne, eager to oblige.
   What can we relish if we recoil
from vulgarity? Not your problem, was it?
   Masterpieces you called "strenuous,"

and were satisfied—or so you asserted—
   with patching up Colette, endless
apprenticeships to other men's disclosures,
   Jouhandeau, Wescott, Cocteau—not "works"

but the launching-pad that sends the rocket up;
   how gleefully you would disparage
or dismiss the monuments I so envied,
   standing emulously in their shade . . .

What *you* wanted—it amounted to addiction—
   was life recounted without design,
without that tyranny—just "the real thing strange":
   letters, diaries, secrets written down,

and not having to dilute or deprave them—
   better one small bold astronomer
than any number of big decorous stars!
   Even silence can be indiscreet,

and not everything we make up is a lie.
About a thousand book reviews
made you too familiar to care much for Fame—
what you liked was how others were moved,

strangers. Your own maneuvers you confined to
the background—more room there than up front
where the young struggle and sweat for their applause
—lovely, though, those intervals of flesh

under hot lights! Such was your *gran rifiuto:*
I wonder if the delicacy
of your domesticities (that son unseen,
that wife dedicated to her art)

made your love for men the mirror type
of mine, you the critical voyeur
resisting "production," I proliferating
among nameless bodies, finding soon

how many were dying who never used to . . .
Granted: you would not write. Then your hand
began to shake so, you could not write. It was
Parkinson's, as we would discover,

but was it not at first a failure of your will?
Those years you passed off as "successes,"
triumphant manipulations of decor;
I recall seasons when you devised

"literaries"—a noun, *voyons*—for our latest
Mme. Verdurin. Besides the fun,
she paid far better than mere authorship, since
the rich, my dear, are always with us.

I sat at those tables with you, glib, grinning,
    ungainly, so greedy for limelight
on my terms and abashed by your forbearance,
    those evenings of unavailing skill.

Silence = Death, according to the slogan
    broadcast for AIDS. Yours was another
silence, as you said with an absurd chuckle;
    a guy can't go on living all the time.

At least it was not the plague, not *our* plague, only
    Parkinson's, only cancer. You smiled,
invoking plausible pretexts—embarrassed
    (such was your humility) to die

among the victims, to benefit even
    erroneously from emotion
reserved for the unwarrantable dead.
    Forty years out of Cleveland, we live

and die in the same Village now, Robert dear,
    and Shaker Heights seems quite as good
a place to have gone from as your Elyria.
    It was the wrong family member

you summoned up: you are the man I should be
    if I had not been the child I was;
not son, not father either, but—I know it now—
    the lost brother found. *Vale frater.*

Theory of Flight: 1908

Dear Gertrude, I was intrigued
to meet Leo's new friend—we read, of course,
    his fantastic farrago
about our Matisse in this year's Salon,
    and though such comparisons
with Carpaccio, etc., seem irrelevant—
    how does "space composition"
account for the flat joy of those colors?—
    far be it from me to impede
the progress of a man with nothing more
    to say for today's painters

    than that the best have only
the originality of incompetence!
    I asked him here for the day:
Matisse always comes for tea and a stroll,
    and has not Mr. Berenson
claimed *in print:* "How very like to mine
    his faculties, his principles"?
Judge for yourself, before that mountebank
    blurs the lens with his scheming
blague: the man is not to be deterred
    (by any regard for mere truth)

from his self-approbation;
at forty, he is sharp as a packet
    of needles, quick as lightning,
and capable of seducing God. Still,
    what happened was noteworthy,
and I prefer that you hear about it
    from me while there is still time—
he has already asked us to I Tatti,
    a visit I rather dread
and greatly look forward to. (Throughout,
    Matisse never opened his mouth.)

Who could help noticing, though,
that Leo's little man looked very well
    down on the beach at Le Mans,
where any shadow casts a seemly spell!
    His white linen suit set off
that sable beard—nor was it hard to tell
    those white shoes were *preconceived;*
and I distinctly detected the smell
    of cloves each time he flourished
his beautiful hands, as if to dispel
    the aroma of the sea.

When I taxed him with dressing,
like women, for effect, he stared then broke
    into the graduated
ecstasy of his laugh, a scale that woke
    edgy echoes from the dunes.
Such vanity is no more than a cloak,
    I suspect, for something worse:
pride is the cure for vanity—no joke
    when, like him, you have never lived

your life at all, just paid it calls and spoke
    French to it with no accent . . .

    But just then a moment came
when one could no longer *parler chiffons:*
    as we passed the Pavilion,
there on the sand lay Wright's contraption (he
    was in Le Mans for a flight,
but his brother's forced landing in the States
    last month had downed him as well—
nothing ever happens when I am there).
    At close range, we could inspect
the machine, which looked to me a matter
    of sticks and string and cheese-cloth.

    And while I was wondering
how such gimcrack got into the air
    or got back down again whole,
our companion—Bernhard the Debonair!—
    gave the thing a vicious kick
and . . . burst into tears! "I cannot bear,"
    he sniffed, wiping them away
with a wonderful white linen square
    produced from *his sleeve,* "to think
how soon this innocent monster will tear
    to pieces the world I love,

    the world of level vision,
or vision from here-below to the heights,
    the world of that privacy
to which our species has enjoyed its rights
    for millennia." By now
his voice betrayed no tremor of what straits
    he had so lately been in,

and I don't believe Matisse (who hates
    any kind of scene) made out
one word. "However the cherished delights
    of the civilization

to which I owe my being
will, in the crannies of Europe, outlast me."
    Back we trailed, no one talking,
to the Delage, poor Mr. Wright's debris
    behind us diminishing
to a forsaken bug. I smother you
    in the details so that when
the little beast declares: "Matisse asked me
    to spend the day—wonderful
hours with his transcendent sagacity!"
    you will have been alerted.

Plus ça change, plus c'est la même
pose, as Matisse says about your Pablo . . .
    And about Signor Popinjay?
I haven't an inkling. All he would say,
    departing, was: *"Il en coûte*
cher pour être raisonnable—écoutez,
    il en coûte la raison." Ask
Leo what it means, I have to spend the day
    with Michael, which means *preparing.*
(A sister for solace, brothers for dismay!)
    Matisse salutes. Love, Sarah.

To a Librettist at Liberty

for J. D. McC.

Frequently an oracle will speak
  from inadvertent altars:
a printing error in *The New York Times*
  suggested—no, *engendered*
the Man-moth, Miss Bishop's urban myth;
  when "soldier Aristotle"
became by a simple slip of the pen
  "solider" (than Plato), Yeats
found himself a philosophical poet;
  and nowanights each diva, prone,
apes unawares the Divine Sarah
  originally peg-legged to
La Tosca's riveting second act . . .

  The situation persists—
our operatic DJ has just played
  what he identified as
Rossini's *Donna del Iago. Gran Dio!*
  Imagine his Lady of the Lake
thus recast—perhaps to compensate
  for Emilia's becoming
(when the Swan of Pesaro *did* attempt
  something like an *Othello*)
no more than Desdemona's upstairs-maid.
  I enjoin this spurious

inspiration upon you: the entire
    tragedy of errors seen

through the eyes of Iago's wife!
    What scenes you will make, what acts
of faith unexplored by either Swan
    (of Avon or Pesaro):
". . . walk barefoot to Palestine for a touch
    of his nether lip"—it sings
itself! And all the more for being
    recommended by the Muse
of Hap, or Mishap, never mind: what is
    the sign of humanity
but making accident the means of art?
    Blind faith is the only kind,
you'll see: Emilia Goes to the Wall . . .

A Beatification

Began with A Moral Tale Though Gay, as bold
as brass, as good as gold, or gilt along
the edges, entitled (*sic*) *The Young Duke*
—"though what," old Isaac d'Israeli wailed,
"does Ben know of dukes?"

Closed on the golden molars of the Earl
of Beaconsfield waving *The Woman in White* away:
"When I want to read a novel, damme, I write one!"
The interval beguiled to great effect
by a Jew *d'esprit*,

or so he claimed: "I am the empty page
between the Testaments"—proving thereby
that only the road of appearances may lead
to the palace of essence. And indeed his least
superficial trait

was his frivolity, which from the first
sank to a considerable depth. Consider then
Chapter Seven of Book Two, which the old fox
could never be persuaded that he wrote:
"I never deny,

I never contradict. But I sometimes
forget." The scene forgotten is the one
where George Augustus Frederick, the young duke,
dresses for a party ("persons of great
consideration:

some were noble, most were rich, all had
ancestors") in something of a rush—
"no time was to be unnecessarily lost
in his preparations (and those of both valets)
for his appearance . . ."

Or for the apparition of a god:
the teakwood dressing-box has been unpacked,
and the shrine for his devotions soon arrayed
with rich-cut flagons of every size and shape
adroitly mingled

with china vases, golden instruments
and the ivory and rosewood brushes, sable-tipped,
worthy even of Reynolds' exquisite device . . .
His Grace was master of the art of dress,
and consequently

consummated that paramount enterprise
with the categorical rapidity of one
whose principles are settled. He then gave
orders with the decision of a Wellington
—the battle was pitched

upon a sparkling plane: ". . . Now let me have
the rose-water—before it dries, you fool!
Light over here, I must have evidence
of how the pores will take another dose
of strychnine. There. Stop!"

The young man's taste was for magnificence;
but he was handsome, and a duke. Pardon him.
Possessed of skin whose pellucid ivory
had never yielded to the Season's strain,
his Grace did not fear

the want of relief ostensibly produced
by a white face, white waistcoat, white cravat.
A hair-chain set in diamonds was annexed
to a glass reposing in the waistcoat seam—
this the only weight

the young duke ever bore. It *was* a bore,
but indispensable. Now it is done.
He stops one moment at the tall pier-glass
and shoots a glance that might have read the mind
of Talleyrand:

it will do! He assumes an air that best befits
the occasion—sublime but cordial—and descends
like a deity from Olympus to dinner below,
the banquet of fortunate mortals who await
an undivulged god.

Had young Disraeli learned the discipline
of being shallow enough for a polite audience?
And Beaconsfield, old, discovered after all
that he loathed the vainglory he lived for,
dyed for, rouged for still?

Good to read the dreadful pages, warmed
by these two words together: *much admired.*
Upon him was bestowed that rarest gift,
the Grace of self-delighting fantasy.
Beatified? Yes,

who shows we must hallow *ourselves* if we are
to enter paradise. No good wishing to be
saints like Joan of Arc or John of the Cross—
"der alte Jude, das ist der Mann,"
as Bismarck observed,

an Image of the Truth, if but the truth
of vanity on the grandest possible scale:
illusion without deceit, solitude without
loneliness. The Young Duke's dressing-table,
a map of Eden.

For James Boatwright, 1937–88

Behold the depths to which we are undone!
A life divided, but only between despised
chores and disparaged cheer—is that a life,
or headlong delay

hanging out till Events enliven the heart?
Enliven? Erase!—then scrawl to lethargy:
the Moving Finger eventually writes off
the hand that needs you.

Gamely you ignored the Greek who maintained
that what he called leisure *(schole)* and school
(what you called labor—found laborious)
were somehow the same;

your classes you valued only for the hours
enfranchised with the once and future young—
the sole lesson learned from such "professing"
was how much longer

youth endures than those who are young assume.
By thirty—you were thirty when we met—
you guessed the closely guarded secret known
to most of the world:

we are not happy, but at least we have
pleasures. Whereof the nightly exercise
—no salt-free regimen, no seaweed baths—
kept you coming back

for more. You had become one of those men
stricken by their maturity as if by
an incurable disease. And then there was
no *as if,* only

the long downward months of which you spent
every moment dying, nothing left
over for the evasions which had been
your lingua franca

(talk is the opium of the healthy).
What the same Greek wrote you heeded now:
the more I am alone the more I am
mythological.

As Keats, who understood, observed,
"until we are sick we understand not."
In time, the vacuum had perfected itself—
teaching? a chaos

of clear ideas; travel? you travelled
about as well as a basket of raspberries;
and love? the arduous pursuit of those
who would not allow

capture or even catching up . . . Was love,
Jim, ever more than a hand poked through
the shower-curtain—a blurred touch easily
rinsed away, laughed off?

Perhaps. For you it was another way
of learning how to stand the loneliness
produced by culture, or by culture's dreams.
So can dreams come *false,*

old friend, for there has been too much
shaving of the cedar-wood round the lead—
the lead itself powdered away at last,
the pencil pointless.

You went with a sigh of relief—to me a sign
that any past we might hope to reclaim
spreads like an oil slick, wide behind us,
and the oncoming

years of retrieval diminish even now
until our name becomes, to memory,
a synonym for weaknesses endured,
or worse still, adored.

After K452

In conversation, even
determined admirers could discover
"absolutely no sign of unusual
powers of intellect, and almost no
    trace of culture"; Ludwig Tieck,
prompted to rekindle impressions cold
some fifty years, contrived to produce
for listeners longing to be misled,
    no more winning depiction
of the Meister he had famously known
than these infamous words: "he was small, swift
of movement, with a stupid expression."
    Centuries on, we have made
him out to be giddy, extravagant,
and judging from his letters (even to
his mother!) gratuitously obscene . . .
    Gleeful though, positively
exultant when it came to his exploits:
"I personally regard the quintet,"
he wrote from Vienna to Leopold,
    "as the best thing that I have

    so far composed in my life."
He would compose things farther in that life,
but "so far" puzzles. How much did he know,
this master of time, or how ignorant
    could he be at 28?

Soon he would fall much too ill not to have
all the symptoms of perfect refinement—
though anything but "refined," nor ever
     be sufficiently "adult"
to remain unproductive for the next
(the last) seven years—though how difficult
he would find it to be shallow enough
     for a polite audience!
But I believe he knew what he had to make,
and when the solitude would cease. The worst
thing about his death was the disrespect,
     vulgarity, meanness . . .
God should have arranged for Mozart dying
to vanish—dissolve like a puff of smoke!
(One among many pieces of advice
     I could have passed on to Him.)

Culture and Its Misapprehensions I

for Hanna Loewy

She smokes too much, my Viennese friend; what's more
her vision is bad and her occlusion worse:
she cannot set her sights, or her incisors,
higher than headlines, harder than steak tartare.

Given, even so, to insight, to appetite,
she reads not my poems but their titles, as
likely as not to divine from the bold-face
letters some sense of whatever I may write.

Which system sufficed until, a week ago,
a lyric appeared with the problematic name
"After K452," whereupon she became
eloquently vexed that I had left her no

clue, or too many clues, and taxed me thus
(roupily gasping through a toxic pall
of her own): "At first I thought you meant Bhopal—
the Union Carbide formula—and I was

bewildered (both of us know that Relevance
is hardly your thing), but then I realized
that acronym must be the one devised
in France for a new AIDS drug—until 'France'

reminded me of the cryptogram for their own
abortion pill we're not allowed to import—
or was 'K452' the plane on Red Alert
over Korea that *had* to be shot down?

At last I guessed it: none of the above,
but call-numbers of a dial-a-sex line
(spells JISM or something), premonitory Sign
of the Times when only surrogates are safe . . ."

Not until that point did I manage to stay
the resourcefulness of her surmising flow:
"Hanna dear, it's a Mozart quintet, you know
the one—for woodwinds and fortepiano—K

452." And provisionally the swarm
of horrors and catastrophes abated
in favor of the Koechel-enumerated
genius who never did the world much harm.

Culture and Its Misapprehensions II

Assigned by *The Manchester Guardian* to "court coverage,"
James Agate divulged to his diary *Ego 9*
how the wife of an architect twice her age had been
the mistress of her chauffeur who was *half* her age;

a hammer had done for the husband, swung by the wife
or the waif. Both lied, but their alternating claims
enlivened the case, each suspect shoring up blame
out of the other's shrift, as if for dear life . . .

As Agate observes, theirs was not an original doom,
but plainly the work of some great French *prosateur:*
the fact that she slept with the newly debauched chauffeur
night after night, and her six-year-old son in the room

(the husband apparently nonchalant in the east wing),
was Balzac *craché.* And the horrors she talked in the box—
exactly the way Emma Bovary always talks.
One flagrant detail in her evidence: hoping to bring

her husband round, she happened to step on his dentures
and then tried to put them back into his mouth
so he could speak to her. Pure *(sic)* Zola. Truth
no longer figures here, and only fiction ventures

to account for our credence. By the time the episode
appears *("Cause Célèbre")* on *Masterpiece Mystery*
I can no longer unravel the human history
from all its narrative snarls. As for the coda,

once the boy was sentenced to die (time after time
she was asked: "When your lover came to your bed and revealed
his deed, what was your first thought?" until she wheeled
on her accuser and shouted: "To protect him—

O my God, my first thought was to protect him!"
Henri Beyle would have called such a thing sublime)
and the wife acquitted, she stabbed herself six times
on a riverbank, and toppled in, and drowned. Effective?

Not until some layers of chronicle can weave
a credible cocoon around what we take for real . . .
Humanity has always been the story-telling animal
that must lie to itself in order to believe.

Culture and Its Misapprehensions III

We know it is not art that teaches us to love
correctly (evidence from any old death camp
invariably includes those Schubert fans who prove
to have enjoyed the most lamentable taste in lamp-

shades). But still we attach our fondest reliance to
moral consistency, once we manage to stave off
hopes that the baddies always welter in *mauvais goût;*
familiar as we may be with a slob who adores Chekhov,

we find it hard to grant an historical evil-doer
downright humane impulses of intimacy and charm!
Who would you say is speaking like this (in 1584):
"The apricots have arrived, but alas in such a form

that had you not apprised me, I should never have known
what they were. And tasting, for certain been taken ill!
Yet how good they must be, from the espalier grown
below your south gallery . . . I believe the yellow jonquil

they brought you from Aranjuez is a wild flower, one
that blossoms sooner in the fields than in our park,
though not so fragrant . . . Clara's captive is surely no heron—
she writes that it is very small, more like a lark . . ."

Thus the Spider of the Escorial, Felipe el Rey,
whose letters from Lisbon to his daughters I translate
(rhymed hexameters permitting); and written that same day,
a sentence he could not only countenance but create:

"that the heretic's right hand be severed with red-hot iron,
that in six places his flesh be torn from the bones by pincers,
that he be quartered still alive, his heart then to be torn
from his breast and flung in his face." The king then answers

inquiries about one of the dwarves on the royal staff:
"Magdalena's fondness for strawberries is as immense
as mine for nightingales, though of these I hear few enough
and only from my southwest windows." Ah, painstaking prince!

your diabetic gangrene could not for one moment be dressed
by so much as a wet cloth, and after fifty-three days
of agony you died uncomplaining to the last . . .
Yet nightingales, apricots, a jonquil from Aranjuez,

the Infanta's espalier, and Magdalena's appetite
must figure in that ever-to-be-reopened chronicle
of what it is to be human, not only to exhibit
Prescott's "unnatural monster" but also to tell

his daughters "your aunts have not at all shortened their bustles
which are terrible, save for those of Doña Graciosa."
Unnatural acts are assigned to many, but it is always
nature which has shown—even by concealing—the way.

The Victor Vanquished

for Tom, 1989

At the going rate, your body gave you
—made you—too much pain for you to call it
yours. Oh, not the pain, the pain was all yours

and all you had; by the end you hugged it
closer than their anodyne substitutes:
pain was your one religion, pain was bliss.

But this body, where almost everything hurt
and what didn't hurt didn't work—*yours?* Never!
Like anybody's, it gave nothing up

that soap and water couldn't wash away.
Whose was it then, this desecrated pond
where all fish die, where only scum persists?

Anybody's. Nobody's. Like a king
who keeps recognizing as "my people"
the rebels who have pulled him off the throne . .

Your body not your body. What about
"your" friends? We want playmates we can own.
Could these be yours? Since every friendship

grows from some furtive apotheosis
of oneself, who were these dim intruders
presuming they inhabited your pain,

as if there could be room for them as well?
You would not have it—let them all go hang!
For two years, the body alone with its pain

suspended friendship like the rope that holds
a hanged man. All you wanted was to drop
this burden, even if it meant that you

would be the burden dropped. And "your" lovers?
What about love—was it like "your" disease,
an abnormal state of recognition

occurring in a normal man? Love is
not love until it is vulnerable—
then you were in it: up to here in love!

The verdict of their small-claims court: it takes
all kinds to make a sex. Had you made yours?
Everything is possible but not

everything is permitted: in love
you were a shadow pursuing shadows,
yet the habit of the chase enthralled you,

and you could not desist. You would make love
by listening, as women do. And by lying
still, alone, waiting. You did not wait long.

Life in general is, or ought to be,
as Crusoe said, one universal Act
of Solitude. You made it death as well.

Visitations

You are my last hope, doctor.
"Nobody but Sir Oliver Lodge,"
they said, is likely to do something for me,
       although it was not "for me"
I wrote the Society seeking
a referral (yours was the one name given);
       nor is it principally
on my account that we meet today
in your rather charming and altogether
       reassuring office: no,
I am not the one who is . . . needy
(Have I got it right? Is that your word for what
       I mean? *Bedürftig,* we say)—
it is my husband who *stands in need*
(there!) though he would be reluctant to admit
       any such thing. Nor should I
have sought this interview for myself,
supposing I had been the star and not just
       a supernumerary
in our "drama" (which to you may seem
no more than just another case history). . . .
       Harley Street is a long way
to come, and if specialized succor
was all I required—medical solace, yes?—
       why, Munich has resources
more than adequate to the distress

of a woman whose marriage is apparently
      waning. . . .
                 I gather you are
   among the rare physicians concerned
with Occult Research—one must come to England
      to find such a conjunction—
   and I tell the mortifying tale
of my husband's Altered Circumstances and
      their effects on our marriage
   and myself, with a presumption based,
as I began by saying, on the fond hope
      that you are . . . that you may have . . .
   Doctor, I am in desperate straits!
Do you think, once you have heard the story
      out, that you can possibly
   help my husband and thereby myself?
Of course I realize that to mere reason,
      his situation is mere
   fantasmagoria and self-abuse—
no, in English that is not at all my sense:
      self-delusion, I should say—
   but surely life affords occasions
when reason will not do to accommodate
      the facts . . .
                 Yes, I am coming
   to it, what you call *the point,* although
nothing so distinct, nothing so sharp, you see,
      is in my grasp. Bear with me,
   dear doctor, soon I shall have managed
to conquer my shame (that is what it is:
      shame) and you can determine
   whether there is some treatment *for him,*
or I must return to Munich and . . . my life.
   I have been married three years

to Herr Willi Schneider: does the name
ring a bell? No? No bell? Suppose I had said
    Willi-and-Rudi Schneider,
  the celebrated clairvoyant twins
sponsored by Baron von Schrenck-Notzing. . . . I see
    you know whom I mean. It is
  unlikely that a specialist so
initiated as yourself in these
    Mysteries would not.
                  For me,
  however—and I seem to have been
the one woman (one person!) in all Munich
    about whom you could say this—
  no such recognition occurred, no
willing delight in his notoriety
    welled up in me to define
  the man by his singular talent
(albeit one that was fraternally shared). . . .
    For me, you must understand,
  Willi Schneider, from our first meeting,
was a man—no more than that, indeed no less:
    a perfectly charming man
    (only a bit too conscious, perhaps,
of being so) with sharp features, sapphire eyes,
    and a continual smile,
  in speech as in silence. The brother,
the *twin,* made his appearance soon afterwards,
    eager to bewilder me
  with Perfect Likeness, but I held fast
to my lover's "imperfect" identity;
    nor was I ever in doubt
  (as so many claimed they were,
positively gloating over the sameness,
    as if the Uncanny was

implicit in the mere existence
of apparently interchangeable twins!)
         —I swear to you, I never
     faltered for a moment as to which
sibling would be my life's companion and which
         a comparative stranger:
     the smile was similar, not the eyes,
which never once deceived me. . . .
                              We met, you see,
         quite unspiritually,
     at the annual masquerade-ball
held in Nymphenburg Castle, and through his mask
         Willi's eyes were all I had
     to go on. They took me a long ways. . . .
What happened was hardly unforeseeable:
         an English-and-Eurythmics
     Mistress at the Dalcroze Institute,
readying herself quite amiably to face
         Life as an *alte Jungfer*
     (our merciful usage for "old maid"),
fell violently in love with a younger man
         about whose unlikely gift
     she knew (and wanted to know) nothing. . . .
In German the word *Gift* means "poison," of course,
         though at no time did I think
     of such ominous pedantries then.
The point, Sir Oliver, is that I had not
         heard of the twins' Powers, nor
     did I take much interest in the Beyond—
indeed it may have been just that indifference
         which first drew Willi to me:
     I would go so far as to flatter
myself that by the time we became lovers
         what really united us

was a sort of irresponsible
indulgence in the most literal pleasures
    of the flesh, may God help me!
    and I truly believe that Willi
no longer relished—and no longer *required*—
    what I soon learned to regard
    (with some repugnance) as the psychic's
special powers . . . I have no desire to boast,
        doctor, but what evidence
    I possess compels me to conclude:
it was our lovemaking, in those early days
        —even once we were married—
    that encouraged Willi to escape,
or withdraw, from his career as a medium.
        (Rudi continues with it;
    I hear he is still Receiving Word,
still Making Contact, as those people say, and
        I have no doubt that sinister
    catamite Schrenck-Notzing still provides
the funding for his *Nassträume.* . . .)
                        Sir Oliver,
        forgive me, but I wonder
    if you yourself fathom what is meant
by a successful medium's *special powers?*
        You see, Rudi claimed he had
    much better results if his brother
continued to practice as well, and it was
        only after a series
    of quite unproductive séances,
by which time I had of course become aware
        that Willi made a living
    out of Things the other side of death
(and I assure you I took no part, myself,
        in such diversions), that he

confessed, with some show of reluctance,
—as if sorry to implicate me in this—
     that his communication
with the Other Side relied on
ungewollter Samenausgus, sexual
     expenditure without which
his capacity to Make Contact
seemed to be compromised. So on the eve of
     each séance there was to be
no more lovemaking . . .
                                        I assure you,
doctor, this divided claim upon Willi's
     appetites—or aptitudes—
was not contested by me, but as
the months passed, there became apparent
     —apparent *to him,* you see—
an imbalance in the two kinds of
experience, his ever-rarer embrace
     of a living woman and
whatever . . . ectoplasm it was that
left his underwear . . . *klebrig* afterward.
     First gummy, that is your word
for *klebrig,* no? then stiff—any wife
observes such things. And wonders. And deduces.
     As I said, Sir Oliver,
Willi's circumstances have altered:
he now believes the "relations" he has had
     with these Others are not just
necessary to his powers, but are
superior *in kind* to those he has with me,
     flesh of his flesh! if the phrase
is not, in this context, ironic
to excess . . . Nor do I altogether doubt
     his contention. Who can claim

to be the arbiter of someone
else's ecstasy? I acknowledge my own
    —it is as a physician
  I confide in you, Sir Oliver—
to be perhaps oversensitive, perhaps
    over-responsive to appeal.
  It reminds me. . . . Indeed, you may know:
we have in Vienna a sort of humorist
    who offers his aphorisms
  in a little paper he publishes
himself, scurrilous sayings but often sage;
    the sagest occurs to me
  with all the incontrovertible
application of hindsight. How easily
    I grasp its bearing now:
  "A woman is, ocasionally,
quite a fair substitute for masturbation.
    It takes, to be sure, a strong
  imagination." . . . You can see why
the words stay with me, doctor. It is my fate
    to have married a man whose
  imagination is inhuman,
and Powers beyond my presence have prevailed.
    Oh, I am certain they come
  quite unassisted—no self-abuse
involved (there, that time it is the right word, no?). . . .
    I keep harping on my hope
  you can help me overcome what lies
Beyond, Sir Oliver, for in the light (or
    darkness) of your eminence
  there abides some notion. . . .
                    An Officer
of the Society for Psychical Research
    may be possessed (forgive me!)

of certain practices which a mere
doctor might overlook . . .
                    No such thing:
                                no word?

        no use?
                    I must abandon
    all hope of what to you, I suppose,
are merely supernatural formulas.
        But is it too much to seek
    from you such tactics as might restore—
or does the fault lie closer to home:
            lie with me? Am I wanting?
        Do not humor me, Sir Oliver!
A true assessment of my own powers . . .
        At least if you assured me
        that this . . .
                        Permit me to expose what
realities Willi has forsworn. . . .
                                Convince me

        mine are worthy. . . .
                        Consider
        these . . . manifestations!
                            There now! So:
I am reassured, and our—may I say, *our?*—
        exertions enable me
        to restore a vanity vital
to any continuing life—eurhythmics,
        you recall, has been my line
    of work (this was evident, perhaps?)
and now I have been . . . substantiated by
        its lessons, as if I could
        recoup certain losses . . .
                        You need not
ring for the nurse, Sir Oliver, I can dress

myself without assistance,
and your office is near the cab-stand.
To Munich I shall now return, dispossessed
    of hope as of illusion.
    Yet as a woman of parts, you have
given me some reason to regard my age
    as not entirely tragic . . .
    No, by "my age" I meant my *years*. Still,
to be a good quarter past the century
    is quite as bad as to be
    thirty-five. . . . As you see, I am too
impatient to wait until temptation comes
    to me, doctor. Grim though your
    prognosis is, I thank you for it—
for everything. What a relief, doctor,
    that the time has come to pay:
    in all professional services,
only the fee is exactly what it seems. . . .
    How tonic, reality!
    I feel quite launched on a new career,
to which we need not attach any new names.
    The old ones are so apt, no?
    Only Willi could do better than
"Fallen Woman," being himself a risen man.
    Good evening, Sir Oliver,
    I hope you will take it as no mere
formality if I say *wiederseh'n* as well . . . ?

Undertakings

Though "a spindle-shanked withered virgin"
    (my source is Virginia Woolf),
Rose Macaulay was right about ruins;
    perhaps it takes one to know . . .
She said it best in her obvious
    phrase: the *pleasure* of ruins.

We are not aggrieved by the wreckage
    of Selinus; we inspect
the unrestored stanchions of Sayil
    without despair, without dread:
these places reward our intrusion
    by a sense of victory,

partly ours for Being There with them,
    partly theirs for surviving
to greet Us. Anything real can give
    human beings pleasure; pain
inheres only in what has not come
    to pass, the unmade event,

as when we read, in Baudelaire's list
    of *petits poèmes en prose*

projected and not written: "Captive
   in a Lighthouse," "Festival
in a Deserted City" . . . Suffer these
   ruins of what never was.

For David Kalstone, 1932–86

What became of him after the cremation? . . . Below David's
windows, Maxine took a small vial from her purse and emptied
it into the Grand Canal. . . . Into the tidal river just east of
Stonington I emptied the white gravel of our friend. . . . A last
teaspoonful had been saved to mix with earth.

—James Merrill

My own stake in his story had been pulled up
    years before such benignly recounted
elemental emptyings, comminglings; and
    wisdom asserts it is delusional
folly to dwell on the past. Well past sixty,
    I know little more about wisdom now
than we did at thirty, but lots more about
    folly, and of course I tell what I know—
the mind makes itself by making rules; the facts
    insist on exceptions . . . Fact: his ferry

crossed the bright Lagoon a dozen years ago
    leaving Palazzo Barbaro behind
with all the drastic ease of "Life" in Venice—
    a more exuberant mundanity
than he was born to in McKeesport, achieved
    in Lowell House tutorials, or had
thrust upon him (easy mark!) by Manhattan:
    "living Beyond Reproach is well and good,

Richard, but it would be nicer if the place
    were just a few blocks closer to the Park!"

I met his boat in Padua, where we gave
    one another the warm shoulder (buggers
can be choosers), both of us electrified
    to be so literally Out To Lunch,
as our correspondence of the seventies
    (relinquished from "the files" by his estate)
makes evident we were, gaiety welling
    thin and fast . . . I instance this encounter
—far from our last, though the last to reward
    contested attachment with an image

worthy of his powers—for the symbolic
    rection of the thing: just where I dreaded
drenching (or drowning!), immersion anyway
    in the littoral drift, I would see him
with one tactful butterfly-kick scoot across
    our social shallows to the next tide-pool.
This spawned a certain unmerited scorn
    (had I not longed to escape the very
marination he so madly plunged into?)
    and it is only justice to invoke,

for tonic fun of my funerary picture,
    the spectacle of David emerging
out of the fiery Venetian furnace,
    blinking, sun-blind, in his genial mood
of acquiescent panic. As Jane Austen says,
    "a mind lively and at ease can do
with seeing nothing, and can see nothing
    that does not answer." Witness my friend
traversing the lagoon to make I-contact . . .

Which deeps have now been further dimmed
by a vial of surreptitious cinders
    poured from a gondola by prudent friends
to join the Dreck of Ages; more recent swill
    discolors the ashes off Stonington;
and dark as the Styx, from my vantage, is the Charles
    where decades ago in Cambridge we first
discoursed upon the Theory of Desire—how
    evaded, how endured—happily trudging
to the grave of Henry James (DK leading,
    blinking hard against the light that failed

to blind him only because he was half-blind
    already)—the sun off the river fierce
on an afternoon of transcendental snow,
    obeisance to that great garrulous Shade
the one sure thing our tentative hearts could share.
    So much rope we accorded each other,
the reverence of certain figurations,
    certain forms by fond artifice achieved:
Balanchine and Bishop and the creator of
    Merton Densher. "Denture, David? Didn't James

for once bite off less than he could chew?" "My dear,"
    he rounded, "I'm glad you said that to *me*"—
art was always an unpersuadable justice
    done to the world, and contemplation
of poems indeed the temple undestroyed.
    . . . Dear discerning critic, now that all change
has been put past you, now that even *your* eyes
    could find, as in a glass clearly, the Forms
of Loss, I wonder—can we be reconciled
    to affections that started with a stone
and ended at sea, all the makings we most

valued apparently *insoluble?*
Winnowing those letters of mine you kept (Why?
    Can I have corresponded *to* the man
who wrote them and *with* the one who read them first?)
    it seems to me I missed an easy clue
by ignoring a mutual friend's remark:
    "the True, the Passionate Kalstone comes out
at the Bechstein . . ." That, and one much harder hint
    found in a letter of *yours* from Venice:

"Everything lovelier than it would become,
    Nothing so lovely as it once had been . . ."
But I suppose what divided us *for real*
    was the pursuit of happiness (founded
on forgetting—only wisdom, poor wisdom,
    relies on memory), or what we took
for happiness, erotic hallucination
    which makes the strangest bedfellows of all.
Who could have thought that irregular line-up
    of communicants at the altar-rail

of sex, in which we took our place, would one day
    possess the power to destroy itself?
Perhaps nobody in creation but our old
    deracinated prestidigitator
whose props you so relished in the Palazzo
    until the plague unhoused you even there—
his the imagination of disaster,
    his the genius for following it out . . .
The task has always been what The Master called
    the wear and tear of discrimination

day by day, and ever since you played on us
    that vanishing-trick called dying,
I am left with the consequence of silence—
    it must always be silence *of a sort,*
of course, never zero silence: those last days
    of your undisclosed disease, your silence
made the one intolerable answer . . . Now
    that I live, like most of us, in a world
which has ceased to exist, it will have to be
    your silence I harp on, look to, learn from . . .

What with repeating and forgetting, is it not
    a marvel there can be meanings at all?
Your silence is a sentence I parse, even
    by remembering your loss. Losing,
I realize: meaning consists in trying
    to mean something: there is no other way.
My mind like another Isis gathers up
    your divided ashes, I watch your boat
cross back to Venice and go from less to less,
    vanish into the dark . . . I see you go.

Homage

i

We pay what tribute we can—of course it is you
who has paid, or who pays now: woe unto you
when all men shall speak well of you (Luke 6:26).

Dear Mr. Howard, I had heard you were coming over.
At present I am living in the country. A dark place
has one advantage: the only possible thing

to be seen, if offered, is a light. *I cannot tell*
precisely when I shall be back in Paris, but
as soon as this is clear I shall write again

and propose an appointment. Thirty years ago . . .
Whatever the weather, your publisher explained,
you would be gardening, or else *au golf,*

whereupon I saw you far out at sea
(I knew you had no car, but perhaps a yawl,
like Mallarmé—what *gulf* in Issy-sur-Marne,

where the fish can't be seen for the weeds?)
until my French recovered. *Meanwhile I look*
forward to meeting you. Much too wet

an April to have missed you on the links—
too wet for flowers, though the ferns rejoice:
with fronds like that, who needs anemones?

ii

One writes, in the end—was it not why you wrote
to me: mere civility from Seine-et-Marne?—
not to say something but Not to say something.

Such was the lesson learned (at least rehearsed)
waiting for Beckett: the missing links between
inscription and erasure, a secret not

an illusion. And still we pester you as I
decades back had done. It is difficult
to get rid of people once you have given them

too much pleasure—particularly those
who are convinced that they possess a key
and will not rest until they have arranged

whatever you wrote into one big lock;
to whom *your* Proust had scornfully remarked:
a work with theories in it is much the same

as a present with the price-tag on it still.
No ideas but in nothing, then,
for my part of the tribute. Happiness

—I guessed as much in 1958—
is no laughing matter. That would be
the other thing. Or would be everything.

What Word Did the Greeks Have for It?

Tendered by Professor Ames, tidings from
    the universe—or at least
from the university (Plato claims
    there is the same difference
between learned and unlearned men as
    between living and dead ones)—

such oracles always come to us clad
    like this in the apparel
of poppycock, and by way of a gloss
    my knowing colleague had scrawled
"yesterday's newspaper is old news, but so
    is today's newspaper—thus:"

Dear Abby, my friend and I are having
    a difference of opinion.
He insists that Damon and Pythias
    were both homosexuals,
I say they were straight. Can you check this out
    and let us know?—Bewildered.

Forestalling Abby, I must first record
        my delight that the two of you
are having a difference—good thinking!
        Our disregard of unity
is every bit as significant as
        our exhibition of it;

provided you differ . . . Precedent compels
        me to ask: What is "straight"?
The danger lies in being persuaded
        before understanding. Let me
instance, *a contrario,* the occasion
        when Gladstone, being informed

a canon of Windsor soon to be made
        a bishop was a bugger,
only remarked, "In an experience
        of fifty years I have learned
that the pagan qualities you refer to
        are frequently possessed by

men of immense erudition, the most
        absolute integrity,
and the deepest religious convictions."
        It *is* bewildering. Myself
I have noticed that when most of us say
        "his heart is in the right place"

we locate that heart rather lower down
        than we care to acknowledge,
and on inspection, the lump in the throat
        is really in the trousers.
Larkin is right: what counts is not to be
        different from other people

but from yourself. There is more repression
    in heaven and earth than is
dreamed of in most psychoanalysis.
    As for that pair in Plutarch,
their devotion seems to have excited
    suspicion even among

the ancients, the same alarm set off by
    Jesus—laying down your life
for another, for all others, appears
    just as suspect as getting laid
by your best buddy. You might tell your "friend,"
    Bewildered, who sounds so sure

of his categories, this much from me:
    the class of men he discerns
is a social, not a biological
    entity. Our genes contain
no instructions as to who is and who
    is not homosexual;

nor do laws of survival require that
    distinctions be made between
the world of the straight and some other world.
    Those whose natures have kept them
at a distance from the community
    cannot appear undefiled

among you without a lurid aureole,
    looking stranger than they are;
they do not need defending—your contempt
    cannot hurt them, they are dark
and love will find them anywhere; nor do
    they need encouragement, for

if they would remain authentic, they must
    live only off themselves, hence
cannot be "helped" without being harmed first.
    Charity begins at home,
but how far does it spread? Where will it all
    end? *Shift, shift, fellatio,*

as Hamlet might have satisfied *his* friend's
    curiosity back then.
These days we cannot let the matter rest:
    Did Franz? Was Walt? Would Vincent? . . .
With a sigh, the unconsenting spirits
    flee to the welcoming shades.

To the Tenth Muse:
A Recommendation

Individual
no longer, but goddess, gimmick, grace, indeed you have been
divided among our needs until all that remains is myth,
        the name we give to

    whatever exists
specifically because it has language for its cause.
Sappho! we descant, and pursuing merely a fond
        ideology,

    our encompassments
of your career and character, however skilled,
however illuminating, like all definitions
        wither their object.

    How much is certain?
Your father's name, your mother's, and that you had three
                                    brothers.
Perhaps you married Cercolas, a rich man from Andros—you
                                    tell us
        you had a daughter,

    whose name was Cleis.
And at least to the ensuing Greek poets you were a Lesbian
in more than a geographical sense. That is enough
        for my purpose here

(one more *use* of you),
which is to curry favor for the candidate *listed below.*
(Most institutions—and you are inveterately said to have
    presided over

    an academy—
request from the sponsor "a brief review of the applicant's major
strengths and weaknesses as a potential graduate student
    and an assessment,

    where possible, of
her stability, motivation, and aptness for working with others."
Forgive if you can the absurd phraseology: these are
    the forms we use now,

    they mean no more than
a touch of the hand, the gesture attempting to remove
the garland which has become a nuisance to the wearer.)
    Ma'am, this is the case:

    Lynda Schraufnagel
who died last January of lymphocytomatosis
would tolerate my classroom in order to show cause
    for later parlays

    chez moi concerning
the unsuccessful poems she had managed to produce
and the ones to be attempted now that those were behind her,
    shocking recitals

    of what to me seemed
an inordinate life if it was to be imputed
to the decorous catechumen watching me from my sofa.
    I mourn her, although

it is difficult
to justify my grief (for if mourning needs no excuse
the way we live—and die—now, it still has to elbow out
    stiff competition):

during those sessions
I had not been, or had not succeeded in becoming, despite
the intimate hours we pored together over her verses,
    an intimate friend.

Whatever it was
I happened to "know" about Lynda she had confided to poems,
and only the poems to me (the nuance won't have escaped you
    —you of all people).

Angular, graceful,
her manic glee in assuming the mask of a scornful dyke
deceived me about her age—I thought she was a *girl*!
    She was forty-one

when she died, just now,
but a coltish ease in each movement reinforced the style
of adolescent insouciance I attributed to her grins . . .
    I would discover

she had been married,
yes, but he was a transvestite; she had greedily abused
every substance in the book, *yes, but she was no reader;*
    the nuns had taught her

to bear the ennui
of almost any routine she would be faced with, *yes, but
now she knew how eagerly she had welcomed victimization.*
    No matter what chore—

 bank-teller, waitress,
student-teacher, even the tedium of my assignments—
could be sucked into her secret knowledge: *women are dupes!*
 They let men have them

 to avoid having
themselves. And that's where you come in, Ma'am, taking up
the slack to have your say, your way, now that Lynda
 is beyond my help

 (which she put up with)
or any assistance from decorous sources (which she despised).
I don't mean to darken counsel (who could advise Sappho!)
 but if, in your lost

 inimitable
manner of speaking, you were to resume where we left off,
you might explain that sexual attraction makes the strangest
 bedfellows of all,

 that to surrender
oneself for anything but desire is to destroy that part
of oneself which from the first enabled (or compelled)
 one to surrender.

 So much of her life
seemed a longing to *get lost.* Perhaps you could,
in death, convince her about finding. Genius alone
 can afford to vex

 itself as she did
without suffering injury. She suffered. I make
no such claim for Lynda Schraufnagel the poet, the woman.
 Merely I observed

in her (and with her
in myself) that our deepest desire aims at transformation.
Now that she is past changing here, with us, Ma'am,
    I leave it to you.

. . . Et Dona Ferentes

for Eleanor Cook

About offering they were often wrong-
headed, these two modern masters; about
receiving too—perhaps that accounts for
why they are masters;
                      genius, after all,
is related to disregard, a dour
sort of attribute engaging neither
human heart nor angelic grace, just
divine apathy.
                  Take, for example,
that business of a Latin lexicon
given—on what pretext, what premise?—by
Wallace Stevens to Robert Frost one March:
"Rather than sending
                    my copy, I shall
procure a fresh one for you and mail it
to Key West, where you can look up such things
as *lotus eaters,* and so on." Always
a deliberate
                matter with Stevens,
procuring lasted well into July:
"Not, as I had thought, the Liddell & Scott
(they confined their attentions to Greek) but
the Lewis & Short—
                  I have had to send

to England for it. Nonetheless I hope
its occasional use will yield as much
delight to you as it has given me."
Frost was 61
                    and still to Stevens
(by five years the younger man) "Mr. Frost."
Odd that Key West should constitute a tryst
for these two Northern Spies—it must have had
everything to do
                    with "lotus eaters,"
but why a *Latin* dictionary then?
Weren't they Greek, the Lotophagoi?
The occasion strikes me as historic,
mythical—fraught with
                            symbolic portents
for any future poetry, the way
meetings between monarchs once signified,
after ritual gifts had been exchanged,
new frontiers imposed,
                    whole populations
henceforth compelled to speak another tongue . . .
The episode (but what did Frost send *back*?
Seven years later he was "Dear Robert")
figures tellingly
                    in our chronicle
of culture, the muzzy *chanson de geste*
whereby we may recognize, however
disputed the phrasing, the figures of
What Is Remembered.
                    I translate freely:
Wallace the Wily, Lord of Qualified
Assertions, did to Duke Robert, Dynast
of Dogmatic Doubt, deliver—feeling
himself adequate

among the orchids
but a lost soul in the kitchen-garden—
the ceremonial key, the Gift Proper
"in the porches of Florida, behind
the bougainvilleas" . . .

After lunch, His Grace
recalled that the Bible says to forgive
our enemies, not our friends—"Is there not
a touch of vulgarity, Stevens, in
any reward, for

anything, ever?
If you're given champagne at lunch, there's sure
to be a catch somewhere. Honor among
thieves, I think, is complicity in crime."
And just about here,

when neither poet
was taking the hint of an ignorance
he never knew he had, would be the place
where a neutral text, say Ovid (upon
which each paladin

might feel himself
god enough to descend to the sons of men)
came in handy for the polite consensus
much needed now, along with a napkin
and a kindly nap.

Thence the lexicon
was but a natural move, like a man
reaching for a glass across the table.
"Do let me send mine to you, Mr. Frost . . .
With it one opens

eyes of the living
gently as one closes eyes of the dead."

To which Duke Robert, looking at Wily
Wallace as if he were an intensely
musical cobra
              caught listening to
the snake-charmer's flute, was heard to reply
(but who was there to preserve such words dropped
from the eaves? The chronicle submits):
"You speak as you write,
                          Stevens, in patches
of deep purple. If Latin were a bridge,
I should prefer to swim. But I enjoy
your generous offer—I'll put myself
back to school for you."
                    "With me, Mr. Frost—
school is merely the continuation
of politics by gentler means; surely
we are together as politicians,
if not as poets?"
                  "Who knows what we are
as poets?" And the two laughed, with that tact
which is the capacity to engage
the egoism of others. How one broods
over that encounter
              of 1935;
henceforth, according to the chronicle
—the Golden Legend and the Leaden too—
relations diminished to the point of
becoming lasting.
             No more offerings
are recorded, and no theory of
reception advanced. As if they neither
expected nor could resist rebuttal,
we leave the poets
                 equally enforced,

avoiding the odd advantage as
savoring too much of a conclusion.
Meanwhile the Latin dictionary lies
there. *Tolle. Lege.*

Telemachus

She could have been my aunt, she looked a lot like those
fragrant ladies who hugged me when they visited:
    friends of my mother's
I learned to call *aunt*—why not Aunt Helen as well
    as all the others?

Of course I knew they were not the same as *real* aunts:
they would laugh and ask the silliest questions, but
    at the mere mention
of what I wanted to do once I was "grown up"
    they paid attention.

This one listened like that. She looked so much . . . taller
than any of them, it was odd I never gave
    much thought to her size;
perhaps because she moved so little. The sunlight
    seemed to hurt her eyes

—she was sitting in the one spot on the terrace
where the canopy produced a corner of shade:
    the afternoon sun
in Sparta is ruthless as Egypt's (she explained)
    in any season—

and she had wrapped a purple scarf around her head,
casting a purple shadow so I couldn't see what
    color her eyes were.
Everything she wore was purple, though, or
    maybe lavender,

even the amethysts in her rings—like purple eggs.
And yet she must have been watching me as she lay
    back on the chaise-longue
sipping her stinger (sunlight through the awning made
    the drink look all wrong,

as if coals, not ice-cubes, were in the glass), for though
she had never seen me before in her life, or in mine,
    she knew me, she said,
because she had known . . . my father: "you have the same
    mouth, the same shape head,

and the way you blink your eyes is the same . . ." Funny,
just then I noticed *she* never blinked, only stared
    as if she could see
what? What no one else even suspected was there,
    something behind me,

or maybe still to come. "You'll find him, don't worry,
you can't lose a man like that. Of course you can lose
    yourself, and you will:
that's what finding a father means." And she ordered
    the servants to fill

my pack with presents—"souvenirs of the old days,"
she said smiling—among them a silver wine-bowl
    that had been inscribed
For the Wedding of Paris and Helen, except
    those names had been rubbed

out and *Telemachus and Circe* etched instead
(it would be years before that meant a thing). For now,
    there was another
journey: I must return to Ithaca—no use
    arguing with her.

"I've seen it already. I know. Nothing happens—
it never happens, it only is. Your mother,
    your island, even
that immortal witch whom your father bequeathes you,
    all will be given

because like me you will return. Go now. Power
is the ability to lose." And fell silent,
    actually fell
asleep while I was still beside her—a long heap
    of lavender wool,

glossy amethysts, and a sort of sour sighing
were what remained of Aunt Helen. I took the bowl
    and all the other
presents down to the harbor and sailed home to wait
    there for my father.

"Lives of the Painters—
Artists' Antidotes"

It was a compilation I should have
or have a look at: *Artists' Antidotes*
was the title, and you were confident
stacks of them were still on hand, Towering,
Stranded—wherever that kind of art-book
is remaindered ("art-book," of course, in quotes).

I disavow all such similitude:
there never was an opus of the kind
you put me wise to, visionary friend!
I could tell just by turning the pages—
no book *like that* has ever existed,
open the damn thing anywhere you like:

why not begin at the beginning with
"The Artists of Lascaux"—simple enough,
the antidote is *breathing*! No more than
the regular action of human lungs
suffices to reduce all images
to vague discolorations in the cave.

Leaf through halfway, to the marmoreal
composure of David's Horatii
taking their oath like helmeted Rockettes—
the antidote is plainly *moving:* flinch

a hairsbreadth and the frontal episode
dishevels at the seams. Once we have come

to the last of your singular book, turned
almost all the pages (art at an end)—
the antidote to Twombley's Apollonian
graffiti is *writing:* to unpeeled eyes
any cacography will serve, any
signature supplant these wavering signs . . .

But was it ever difficult, my friend,
to find a distinguished cure? Who has failed
to come up—merely by aspiring To Be—
with a devastating put-down of art?
Your book, wherever we look, is rife
with artists' antidotes: the verbs of life.

"Man Who Beat Up Homosexuals Reported to Have AIDS Virus"

—The New York Times, March 8, 1991

to the memory of Alan Barnett

To *The New York Times:* Your health editor
may not print this; my social-worker says
    it will do me good
to write it anyway, and in my case
the terminal treatment has to be truth.
    Not much else, by now,
can "do me good": the hospital routine
laboriously contends with new bouts
    of pneumocystis,
thereby bestowing leisure to survey
my escalating KS lesions—caught
    red-handed . . . Last week
you ran an article about a man
whose name you withhold, though his age agrees
    with his appearance
when I was in his hands, and he in mine.
This was years ago, long before there was
    a reason to think
such handling was red, or led to being dead!
I can identify him all the same,
    though all different
from actions in which he says he took part.

—If he took part, then which of us took all? ,
    For all was taken,
as you report: I am one of the "many
gay men beaten in the 1980's
    by a truck-driver
in the New York area," and I owe
myself whatever account I can give
    of that episode.
It is not the reason I am here, nor
is my being here the result of it—
    but it represents
one dimension of the life I am in
a final position (no evasions!)
    to evaluate . . .

*Maureen, it's Jane. Did you get the clipping? If you read it through, you
realize why I* had *to call . . . No, now. We need to talk. You put things
off, they just get right back on and ride you worse. It has to be Jack, Sis,*
your husband and the father of your girls! *Everything fits. First of
all about the life-insurance screening—what a way to learn he has that
terrible disease! And then that part about "the large amounts of victims'
blood on himself" . . . Remember how hard it was—well,* I *can remember
your complaining about it all the time—getting those stains out of his
jeans* each week! *It was hard because that was blood—and not from
lugging pork-bellies out of his truck! . . . I don't care what he told you, do
you think I believe what Henry tells me? Of course you're not infected.
How could you be if he hasn't . . . The paper said it's been ten years . . .
Honey, I know: we're middle-aged, thank God! You don't imagine that
Henry and I . . . ? Maureen, you've got to get it through your head there's
something wrong with Jack. And I don't mean his getting sick now—
wrong all the way back. Dumb of me to think the girls would tell you
. . . Sis, do you understand how men get AIDS?*

My social-worker says "we have to be
downright" (she invariably says
    "we" when she means me)
and goes on to assure me that *God is*
in the details—she doubtless heard the phrase
    in her Crisis-Class
("Depression and Dying") only last week.
It could be true, for all I know; there's not
    much hope of finding
Him in the Master Plan. So let's pray
she's right. Herewith the (divine) specifics:
    maybe five years back
I met Mr. X one Saturday night
—more likely it was a Sunday morning—
    as I came around
the corner of Washington and Bethune:
a vision! He was playing with himself
    in the open cab
of a pork-butcher's van—such diversions
are often met with in the meat-market,
    appropriately,
since he asked, when I started cruising him,
if I wanted some. Meat. (I know you won't
    run any of this,
but I'm being downright.) So I went down
on him in the back of his truck. Dark there,
    hard to see—you have
to feel your way on such occasions—but
I found it easy enough to do that . . .
    I found it easy.

Why would *he tell you . . . why tell anyone? A married man with three*
daughters: Maureen, he must have known people would never think . . .
Did he ever think . . . ? And that would make it easy for him to do the

things he did— easier: he was their dad, whatever else he was . . . When did it start? Probably once you and he . . . stopped. Being in New York must have made a difference too. Because New York is different . . . from Nebraska, anyway. I'm not trying to be funny—you always said you hated living there, right up to when they transferred him back here . . . Maybe you knew why, even if there was no way for you to know . . . The paper said he went out looking for . . . the other kind (maybe they weren't so "other" after all) several times a week—you must have thought some-thing even if you wanted not to. Maureen, the paper said "too many times to count"—no, "to remember." And it said the other drivers went out with him too. Does that sound right to you? Sis, when did Jack do things with others? Even beat up queers?

Once he was through, or I was—hard to tell
who it is completes such actions, who is
    active, as they say,
and who is passive (even a woman
is never really passive, I suppose)—
    once our thing was done,
he began talking to me in the dark—
till then, of course, he hadn't breathed a word,
    just breathed, and after
a while of breathing, the usual moan . . .
Maybe my downright talent made him feel
    he could shoot the works . . .
He asked, was that all I wanted to do,
and if it was, would I do something else
    for him. Something more.
He moved around, I knew what he wanted—
it was easy to tell by the clatter
    his belt-buckle made
against the floor. I started to explain
about my "proclivities" (not doing
    what my father did),

and as if, right then, something about *him*
had been exposed, something unbearably
    humiliating,
he began to yell and lash out at me
with that belt. If it was too dark for me
    to guess that my *not*
doing what he needed would enrage him,
it was also too dark for him to see
    where the hell I was:
I managed to slither out of *harm's way*
during the mayhem, and to haul myself
    eventually
out of the *van,* but not before we both
were something of a mess. That was my clue
    to my "assailant"—
there must have been blood, my blood, all over
the place, just as *The Times* reported it.
    All in a night's work.

He claims he hasn't done it in three years: maybe he doesn't need to do it now, but maybe he will. Maybe he has to. Maureen, you've got to trust your own sister: are there times when he takes it out on you? No one talks about beating, but I know it happens in a lot of "happy homes." I'm trying to help you. Listen to me! It could be years before Jack ever shows signs he has this thing—he may keep his strength for quite a while . . . I know you want to take care of him when he's not able to . . . when he needs help. It's a damn good thing you do—at this point I can't see why anyone else would: Maureen, he likes to hurt people! But you've got to take care of yourself first. If it passed into his blood from someone he beat up, what about yours? I suppose that's the only way it could happen now . . . Keep away from him if he—Sis, you know what I mean: if he can't go out for it, what's to keep him from beginning at home, like charity? I'm not joking, Maureen, I just want you to recognize the truth . . . If men are more devious than women it must be because they have more to hide.

But I doubt—being downright—if my man
had much to fear from me—certainly not
    from any of my
blood in any cuts of his, as he told
the Nebraska medical officers.
    I suspect—being
downright and outright—his dose could be traced
to an administration of the same
    bodily fluids
as those I was punished for declining
to provide. Not every faggot who climbs
    into a meat-truck
has my limitations, I know plenty
who would be pleased (*and* able) to oblige
    by humping a hunk . . .
Furthermore—being down and out—I couldn't
care less. I lie here wondering (most days,
    my only life-sign,
unless you count reading *The New York Times*
as a sign of life—and you would, although
    the *Living* section
is sometimes too much for me) . . . Wondering
is what my time is good for—good times! and
    what I wonder is
if the life I have always lived ("always"
being the last 20 years, who could know
    they would be the last?)
was mine at all, my choice—unless it was
just the life I could never acknowledge
    to *The New York Times*
(of course I'm using you as a symbol),
a life so sexually myopic
    I knew only those
faces I had kissed—and not always those!

RICHARD HOWARD

Is this what it comes to? A tribal tale
    of A Thousand Nights
and a Night, except that this Scheherazade
gets herself 86'd . . . Sex turns out like
    reading (believe me
I know whereof I speak—in my corner
the comparison is anything but idle)
    because it gives you
somewhere to get to when you have to stay
where you are. But life is used up, if it's
    used, spent, or wasted . . .

*Mama always used to tell us you get what you pay for. Maureen, that was
a crock! I've learned better, and so have you, by now:* you pay for what
you get. *Jack has to pay, so do you and the girls, Henry and I. The hard
thing is to understand just what he got. Not Henry, Jack! Sis, don't be
dumb . . . I know he got this disease, what I mean is, what did he get out
of what he did that has to be paid for by getting AIDS? Damn right it's
a judgment—isn't everything? I'm not saying he doesn't deserve it, it's
just that if you're going to see him through to the end, you'd better understand the satisfaction—no, it's more than that: the rush, the thrill, or
whatever it is doing things like that to other men could give him. If AIDS
is so awful, then* that *has to have been so good. Do you see? You have to
realize the joy of it if you're going to reckon up the pain. Think about it,
Maureen. I'll call you back once Henry's gone to bed. We'll talk some
more.*

The Times keeps referring to a *life-style*
as having consequences. That is why
    I've made this gesture:
not to dispute your claim, but to insist
the consequences are *not* a judgment!
    This sickness I got
is no sentence passed on my wickedness—

recalling which "wickedness" makes up,
    now as before, most
of what I have lived for. Not died for,
I'm grateful, even to Mr. X . . .
    Why should his actions
incur a verdict, any more than mine?
By the time he reaches whatever wards
    Nebraska affords
(social-worker or not), I hope he can
summon up, as I did, the impulse that
    brought us together
and remembers me. That is what it comes
down to: a matter of remembering
    certain encounters,
certain moments entirely free of time.
I am no longer able to excite
    myself (is that verb
fit to print?), my visions are purely that,
just visions, endless reruns of the scenes
    I have collected.
Remembering is not even the word:
making comes closer. Where understanding
    fails, a word will come
to take its place. Making is my word,
my enterprise. Believe me, I lived through
    such episodes as
the sad one I have described for the sake
of . . . what? Of whatever was exchanged there
    in the dark meat-van
before the end . . . The second half of joy,
somebody said, is shorter than the first,
    and that gets it right.
Whatever's left of my life, I am *making,*
the way I made it happen all along

     —I replay the scenes
from that movie The Past, starring not
Mr. X playing opposite myself
     but Endymion,
Narcissus, Patroclus, all the fellows
I have welcomed to the tiny duchy
     of my bed—the world's
only country entirely covered by
its flag. I thank you for "covering"
     as well as you could
the story to which I have provided
such a lengthy follow-up—gay men do
     go in for length, or
at least go out for it; that is part of
our mythology. And now, perhaps, you
     know another part . . .
The nurse has just come in with another
delicious concoction. The social-worker
     awaits . . . (Name Withheld).

About the Author

Born in Cleveland in 1929, educated at Columbia University and the Sorbonne, Richard Howard has published nine volumes of poetry; for his third, *Untitled Subjects,* he was awarded the Pulitzer Prize in 1970, and a selection from his first eight books was published in England by Penguin in 1991. A distinguished translator of French literature, Howard has received the P.E.N. Translation Medal, the Ordre National du Mérite from the French government, and the American Book Award for his 1983 translation of Baudelaire's *Les fleurs du mal.* His comprehensive critical study *Alone with America: Essays on the Art of Poetry in the United States Since 1950* was re-issued in an enlarged edition in 1980. Richard Howard is University Professor of English at the University of Houston and poetry editor of *The Paris Review.*